A Little Poetry Book

Becky Preston

BookLeaf Publishing

Presentation by *BookLeaf Publishing*

Web: www.bookleafpub.com

E-mail: info@bookleafpub.com

ISBN: 9789357213721

First edition 2023

*To all the beautiful souls who get lost from time
to time.*

PREFACE

These poems are expressions of thoughts, feelings, dreams, imagination and struggles that hopefully resonate with many people.

I found being creative in this way has helped me personally work through so many of life difficulties-some poems of course, are extremely personal, about topics which I have never truly opened up about before. Some poems are just thoughts or observations from other viewpoints. I hope that they bring some hope and peace to anyone reading them, that if you ever feel alone for any reason, you simply are not.

The Queen

Stand tall,
Head up,
Eyes fierce,
Heart kind,
Lips smiling,
Shoulders back,
Confidence,
Unique,
Wild mind,
Spirit is high,
Sexy smile,
Worth-priceless,
Beauty to mesmerise,
Eyes full of glitter,
Heart on fire,
Inner goddess awakened,
Vibe is glowing,
Energy is flowing,
Brain is lit,
This is it.
The Queen

The Questions

The Questions
I am a woman, I've got questions to ask
Answering them is no difficult task
Where are you from? What's your name?
What's your age? Your favourite game?
Do you like popcorn? Salty or sweet?
What's your favourite post workout treat?
Do you like sunsets or sunrise more?
Do you think cleaning is pleasure or a chore?
Do you fall asleep on the side?
 Or flat on your back?
Do you see the world in colour?
Or in white and black?
How do you like your eggs first thing?
Do you cook with a smile? Or like to sing?
What makes you angry?
What makes you sad?
Is me asking all these questions making you
mad?
What's your favourite season?
Is it summer or fall?
Do you like women short?
Or towering tall?
When was the last time you fell tears and cried?
Have you laughed so hard and nearly died?

How do you kiss?
Do you close your eyes?
Do you linger too long enjoying the prize?
How do you react when your buttons are pressed?
Do you yell in a rage or just act depressed?
Where do you want go most on earth?
Somewhere distant or just your home turf?
Do you want babies? Do you want mine?
Or a single life with no family time?
Do you care for riches and nice shiny toys?
Are you a man or one of the boys?
What do you think about sharing your life?
Do you want someone to call your wife?
Are you open? Honest? A gentleman?
Tell me what you can't do and what you can.
Would you dance with me on a Saturday night?
Would you rather be alone during a flight?
Do you believe in aliens?
Do you believe in ghosts?
What three things scare you the most?
How much butter do you put on your bread?
What takes up the most room in your head?
What would you do with your last fiver?
Are you a safe or reckless driver?
Where are ticklish? Or are you not?
Is there something about you, you wish I forgot?

The Watermelon

Oh how relieving
Is the taste of refreshing
Watermelon juice

The Dream

Bronze sun melting into the deep, blue ocean,
Pink sunset and glowing skin
The breeze dancing
Sand grains tickle and cling to legs
While waves gently take the shore in a lingering
kiss,
Palms tall and swaying, smiling,
Dark, dark rum hot and intense
A light heart, and lighter mind,
Feeling free as bird
Stars begin to twinkle and sparkle up high
You search for a planet to see in the sky
The perfect soul
Down on one knee
He utters the word…
Will you marry me?

The War

When you wake up, check the mirror
I want to know if you are any thinner,

You look fatter on your tummy and podgier on
your back,
So, no breakfast for you, you've fallen off track,

I don't think that dress will fit over your hideous
lumps,
Be sure to buy two sizes too big to cover the
bumps,

I checked the calories in that slice of bread,
Way too many, have cucumber instead,

You can have one meal today, salad for tea,
You can't be seen to look too unhealthy,

You look disgusting, you make me sick,
And no, your mind isn't playing a trick,

You have huge hips and grotesque thighs,
I heard someone call you beautiful, trust me it's
lies.

You can't possibly miss a session at the gym,
No one will like you if you aren't perfectly slim,

Your waist must be snatched and ass nice and
tight,
And please do something about that gross
cellulite,

Don't think for a minute you can eat that cake,
Just nibble the edge, that's all you can take.

I know you had chocolate, it's all over your chin,
Spit it back out and right into the bin,

If you get a moment of madness where you think
you ace,
I will come thundering down and wipe that
smile off your face,

Now weigh your cheese and not a gram over
thirty
Your eating is clean, not an ounce of it dirty,

You must overthink every little decision,
I need to make sure I distort your vision,

 Trust me, all the models do this and they look
so much fitter,
I saw it on Insta, Facebook and twitter,

I see you with your friends, checking your every movement,
Is that wine a good choice? You won't see any improvements…

Don't try to fight me, you will never win,
Just like you won't be skinny, slim or thin,

I know I'm hard on you, it's just because I care,
Now put your pretty smile on and pretend I am not there,

Yours truly
Ana x

The Win

You look beautiful today
Just as you are
You are gorgeous this way
Like a shining star

Your smile is magical
It lights up the room
Your hair is fantastical
You own that perfume

You walk with elegance
You are drop dead gorgeous
That killer confidence
No time to be cautious

Yes, pose in that outfit
Choose this look
Please don't doubt it,
Post the pics that you took,

There is nothing to fear
If they stand and stare
Because you are stunning from here
And from right over there

You deserve this feeling
You deserve the food
You are growing and healing
So you deserve this mood,

From your lips, hair and glittering eyes
That feature on your pretty face
Your perfectly shaped and sized thighs
You're the hottest thing in this place

Oh girl, you are a beauty Queen,
Breathe out, now breathe in,
A goddess, just own it,
and soak up the win.

The Wolf

I love you she whispered,
I am so in love with your deep, magical soul,
Your rough, strong hands,
Your mind, your goals,

With you, nothing else in the world exists,
My breath taken
My own thoughts adrift,

I'm obsessed she thinks
With the way you stare,
Your hollow back, your fierce glare
Tough bones and tougher muscles,

I need you to love me, she says
Protect me and care
Hold me close at night
I need to have you there,

Maybe I am crazy, maybe just mad,
I'm obsessed, I need you
I always have.

The Mood

The 'Always be kind' is sometimes bullshit,

Some people, when you see them,
they wander up to your door,
It's okay to say FUCK OFF,
Then fuck off a little bit more.

The Fragrance

Coco Chanel perfume,
The smell takes me back
to Northern Cyprus,
Listening to crickets,
And watching for lightning strikes as thunder
cracked in the night sky,
Waiting for Colin the lizard to come along to the
balcony,
Playing cards and learning new games,
The feeling of happiness,
Not a care in the world.

Thank you

The Escape (A sonnet)

I dream so often about being stranded
On an island faraway in the sea
It's covered in palm trees and coconuts
The waves are emerald, turquoise and blue
Calm, gentle, peaceful and beautiful
I lay my sleepy head in a white bed
Underneath the stars I blissfully sleep
I collect sea shells and treasure to keep
I basque in the hot sun like a lizard
I eat enormously perfect passion fruits
And catch fresh, white fish to grill on the fire
I dance freely at sunset, stretch at dawn
I listen to crickets chirp their mad song
I sink my toes into the salty sand

The Unusual One

Marriage doesn't define me,
They said she was odd
A baby isn't the end goal,
They thought how bizarre,

Why aren't you cooking him dinner?
It's most peculiar,
That you're in the gym, stronger than him,
Being your own ruler,

No more fun, time to settle down,
They're strange these women today,
They aren't desperate to stay home,
And look after men every day,

Oh, it's so unusual,
The way she lives her life
It's heart-breaking for me to see,
A woman with strength, ambition and grit,
Standing on her own two feet.

The Moon

Here is the story of the ghostly moon,
The sun will fall only too soon,
And when she does, she will chase her light,
But instead light up the black of the night,

She climbs the jewel studded sky where the stars
aglow,
And casts her magic over the earth below,
She creates an enchanted, solar floor
And watches as magic ignites the poles with
awe,

As comets collide in between dazzling
constellations,
and shooting stars fall in secret locations,
She gazes in euphoria at her celestial land,
And pulls the azure blankets with her gentle
hand,

Her lunar energy guides the wild at night,
Illuminating the way for the bird's in flight,
She gleams her glow for sailors at sea,
Her starry presence shimmering peacefully,

But then and not too soon,
The night will end for the haunted moon,
The sun will climb and turn night to day,
Chasing the midnight galaxies away.

The Addiction

Wake up
Swipe
5 notifications
Swipe and scroll
6 minutes more
Instant gratifications

Zoom in
Zoom out
62 likes on my post.
4 new followers
Even more wallowers,
Who likes my pic the most?

Click
Goes the kettle,
Passcode tapped out
an Instagram queen,
takes over my screen,
Only posting for clout.

Sip the tea
Eat the toast
Oh, their life looks like a dream
A comparison a day

Keeps the smile away
So, appalled at my own regime,

An hour later,
Tap tap tap
The screen lights up her eyes
A tik tok to make
Oh, how incredibly fake
When I photoshop my thighs,

Bed time
Curled up
Body in affliction
To spend the night all alone
Time with my phone
The modern-day addition.

The Magical Mind

There's a list for everything
So many tasks that I find
A million and one things to do
Along with the tabs in my mind,

The sound of someone eating
Chewing is really gross
Ignites a rage inside me
I just can't stand the most,

I've got so much stuff
Everything is a clutter
But don't make a mess with your stuff
Or it will go in the gutter

Going to do the food shop
A hateful task each week
So many people and noises
I want to scream and shriek

Meetings at work
So long and so dull
Wonder if they notice
That I simply can't sit still

So many questions
That I will never ask
Why can't I ever
Just get on with this task?!

I need a new project
Or maybe a new scene
Actually, I'll sort my house out
And maybe a spring clean

Sometimes I sit in a towel
Staring at the end of my bed
It feels like all of the wires
Are tangled in my head

Empathy so strong
I can taste the atmosphere
A sense of who is feeling
Sadness, anger and fear

The weight of the world
Sits on my shoulders
The pressure of my anxiety
Feels like pushing boulders

You will never see this
Its all hidden in disguise
I can't reveal the quirks
Or let you see my lows and highs

This is just a snippet
Of my magical mind
The neurons are electric
A rollercoaster of a kind.

The Reader

I look at her curled up,
Worn out book in hand
Lost in the creased pages
Of a magical land,

I look at her make up free,
Hair messy and wild,
Body engaged with dreams,
A smiling inner child.

The Rant

You know what makes me want to drink,
The stupidity of how people think,
The slowness of a Sunday driver on the road
Suddenly forgetting your iphone code

When people don't know their basic manners,
People with less brain cells than actual spanners,
Adults who can't make grown up decisions,
Adults who have over dramatic reactions,

Fake smiles and faker small talks
Slow people with even slower walks
People who stop in the entrances and just stand
still
Just get out the way, you absolute pill

People who chew really bloody loud,
Then they look all smug and proud,
Cocky arrogant chewing faces,
People who take up two car park spaces,

People who had champagne when you had coke,
Want to split the bill, what an absolute joke
People who ask when are you having a kid
Mind your own business and shut your lid.

The Little Things

The smell of coffee
The feel of puppy fur
Crisp air has it hits your skin through a cracked
window
The last piece of chocolate
The burning crackle of a candle
The stillness of a sunrise
An ice cold drink on a scorching afternoon
The steam from hot tea
A 'Good morning, I love you' text
A 'Let me know your home safe' text
The smell of after sun sinking into sun kissed
skin
A book you can't stop reading
Baby powder
A walk with the dog
Home baked cookies from the oven
Kisses on the forehead
Nights spent star gazing
Pink, golden and beautiful sunsets
White, crisp bed sheets that smell like spring
Pancakes in bed on a Saturday morning.
The sound of belly laughs and shrieks of
laughter
Contentment.

The Moment When

You are looking at the sky,
The twirly milky way above,
Wondering about the moment,
When you fell so hard In love,

The time is still,
No thoughts of back then,
No racing thoughts of what,
how, why or when,

You look at each other
You feel as light as a feather,
It's beautiful and it's bitter,
as it won't last forever.

The Light

I promise when it's intensely dark,
On the nights where black is suffocating,
There are always stars
Sparkling as glimmers of hope,
Always look for them and cling to them,
Never let go,
As long as some nights seem,
And some really feel like forever,
But light will always rise,
The stars will glow brighter,
Your bones will have fight,
And when it does,
It will be so beautiful.

The White Wolf

I have a white wolf,
she is brave and beautiful,
She stands up tall
when everyone else shrinks small,
she isn't afraid of the black night sky,
she stares at the black wolf right in the eye,
He's too mesmerised to howl and he falls,
and my white wolf gently kisses him,
until his black heart thaws.

9 789357 213721